1

Laura & Kharin
I'm so happy I
can share this book
with you.
It is based on the
main part of my
work out in the world –
doing workshops and
seminars for so many
years

Hope you enjoy it

With Love,

Grandma Rose

MEETING YOUR REAL SELF

The Power of the "Not I's"

**Rose Blackham *and*
Keri McGuire**

BALBOA.PRESS
A DIVISION OF HAY HOUSE

Balboa Press books may be ordered through booksellers or by contacting:

Balboa Press
A Division of Hay House
1663 Liberty Drive
Bloomington, IN 47403
www.balboapress.com
844-682-1282

Print information available on the last page.

ISBN: 978-1-9822-5862-7 (sc)
ISBN: 978-1-9822-5864-1 (hc)
ISBN: 978-1-9822-5863-4 (e)

Library of Congress Control Number: 2020922323

Balboa Press rev. date: 11/28/2020

Living A Life
Of
Love, Ease and Joy

Written By
Rose Blackham and Keri McGuire

Illustrated By
Richard Blackham

We Would Like To Acknowledge

"Dr. Bob"

Dr. Robert R. Gibson was known to many people as
"Rhondell"
Born in 1916 & died or "transitioned" in 1994

Dr. Bob maintained that the "Not I" principles
were handed down from teachers
of ancient wisdom.

THE AUTHORS

Rose Blackham is a psychologist and the founder of **Let's Wake Up**, an organization dedicated to the education and study of human behavior and personal growth. She has counseled and developed many programs for thousands of people that include **The Balanced Woman, Abundance and You** and **Circles of Women**. Rose's personal vision and purpose is to assist people in understanding The Power of the "Not I's" concept, in order to create more balanced and peaceful lives. In addition, she has counseled and traveled with many celebrities coaching and teaching these principles. She developed a program called **The Power of Purpose** and taught it to several Fortune 500 corporations including Honeywell, Pillsbury, Colgate Polmolive, Dupont and Wilson Learning Corporation. She credits Dr. Robert Gibson, also known as Rondell, for her profound experiences of positive changes in her own life. He personally mentored and prepared her to teach and pass on this "Not I" information. Later, he gave her permission to teach and write freely about the "Not I's". Rose considers life to be her greatest teacher.

Keri McGuire had the privilege of growing up under the influences of personal and spiritual growth. Being introduced to Dr. Robert Gibson, also known as Rhondell, and the "Not I" information at the early age of fourteen created a journey of personal awakening. She is passionate about sharing these life-changing principles. Her life long career in many aspects of design and writing have given her a variety of creative expressions. Keri facilitated and executed the marketing plans for many of Rose Blackham's successful programs, including **The Power of the "Not I's", The Balanced Woman, and Abundance and You.** She also created and taught a special program designed for young women ages twelve through sixteen called **The You in You**, based on the "Not I" principles and their effect on self-esteem in young women. Keri presently lives in Denver, Colorado where she enjoys her work as an Interior Designer for her own firm.

FOREWORD

Perhaps this book will bring you some powerful information and a new understanding of yourself and your life.

It may be the time to look at your life with new perspectives in order to move toward new levels of clarity and growth.

As long as you are unaware of the harmful conditioning that you learned as a child, you are functioning automatically and mechanically from old ideas and decisions that affect every single aspect of your life. In this book, you will learn what it means to live your life 'awake' rather than 'asleep'. Instead of living a life of conflict and resistance, here you will find the tools to live a life of peace, ease and inner serenity.

Be open to the possibilities…

"Maybe the journey isn't so much about becoming anything. Maybe it's about unbecoming everything that isn't really you so you can be who you were meant to be."

-unknown

INTRODUCTION

Most of us have felt at times that life can be so busy with problems to solve daily along with distractions that can seem endless. Sometimes you may have felt hopeless about it all.

It is not uncommon to experience both good days and some bad days. You may be experiencing health or financial challenges, the loss of a loved one through death or divorce, and other personal challenges which may include addiction or depression, low energy and much more. Perhaps you may be experiencing complications in your personal relationship that just do not seem to improve no matter what you try. It can seem that this is just the way it is and you must accept the good with the bad. And some of you may be walking on your path in search of more light, understanding and purpose believing there is a way out.

Please know that there are answers to dealing with the human challenges that you have had in your life.

Learning to understand that you have a "Real Self" and a "False Self" can totally change your experience of living.

Wouldn't it be wonderful to come from a place of living your life with questions and frustrations to one of solutions and answers? Learning to understand what the problem has been and finding the "way out" can lead you to a life of peace and love.

Some valuable new perspectives about the self as well as specific tools for transformation are given in this book.

Be willing to stay open and experiment with this information to find out if these ideas are true and real for you.

We wish you a beautiful awakened life full of love and light.

CONTENTS

PART I

THE "REAL SELF"
AND
THE "FALSE SELF"

THE "REAL SELF" AND
THE "FALSE SELF"

*I*f someone were to ask, "who are you?" You might answer them by simply saying your name.

Is that who you really are? Or, is that just your name? People often believe that who they are is their name, or career title, or their family ancestry. You have a name, but you are not your name.

The truth is that most people do not know who they really are. You are much more than your name. Let's explore this idea.

You have a "Real Self" and a "False Self". Your "Real Self" is your spiritual self which knows that you are here to love and be loved and that you are good and valuable. Your "Real Self "is pure love and light. This is your divine spirit and connection to God. This is who you really are. When you come to know and understand this truth, you can learn to live a life guided by your spirit and intuition. You will find your life filled with more happiness and joy. This truth of who you really are is pure goodness. This is the truth!

The "False Self" creates all fear and inner conflict. It is the ego, made up of shadows and masks from ideas that you were taught to believe from the time you were very young. This is the part of you that often finds yourself complaining, blaming and defending. This is being asleep.

Here is a jewel of wisdom for you. In every moment you are either connected to your "Real Self" or your "False Self". It is not possible to be both at the same time.

Another way of saying this, is you are either awake or asleep, and coming from either fear or love.

The very best way to find out where you are is to ask yourself "how am I feeling right now?" Your feelings are your guide and indicator. Any feelings of gratitude, love, joy and happiness are telling you that you are in alignment with your "Real Self". Look at your life. Do you feel peaceful and joyful most of the time? Anytime you are feeling like a victim, and experiencing anger, guilt, fear or insecurity, you will know you are asleep forgetting who you really are.

There is good news here. You can choose to change your thoughts at any time. This in turn will create a new feeling, which then changes your experience. You are truly the manifester of that which you are experiencing in your life. Thoughts are things. Feelings are your guidance system to know whether you are awake or asleep. Your life is supposed to feel good to you, and you are in charge of that.

Where you are in your life today is where your thoughts and feelings have brought you. You will be tomorrow where your thoughts and feelings take you.

Are you beginning to understand the value of being aware and in charge of your thoughts? The good news is that you absolutely can do this. It is that simple yet, not always easy.

So, how did you acquire this "False Self"? You certainly would not consciously choose to experience insecurity, lack of abundance, or any harmful emotions in your life, right? You are happiest when you feel good.

Let's take a look at where this all began. By the time a little child is approximately five years old, whatever ways the child was treated by its parents or caretakers became an ingrained belief system. This is the beginning of the conditioning. This is where the creation of the false self begins. This is the creation of the "False Self".

This destructive conditioning is what creates an experience of living life automatically and mechanically based on old ideas and beliefs. This conditioning or "False Self" is actually made up of six individual masked personalities. They have fooled you your entire life into believing that they are your "Real Self". These six masks are called "Not I's". These false personalities influence all harmful thoughts and feelings and create all conflict.

These "Not I's" are the individual masked personalities that become known as the ego.

Up to now this has been the problem. The good news is realizing that they are not real and they are not you. They are the conditioning that has been added on.

In the next chapter you will learn how this crazy thing began.

JEWELS OF WISDOM
"REAL SELF" AND "FALSE SELF"

- The "False Self" creates anger, guilt, fear and insecurity. These are harmful emotions that you were not designed to experience.

- The "False Self" is the ego, made up of shadows and masks.

- Being connected to your "Real Self" is being aligned to who you really are which is pure love and light.

- The "Real Self" is your natural and authentic self.

- Being aligned with your "Real Self" allows your spirit and intuition to offer you guidance in your life.

- The "Real Self" lives with ease.

- The "Real Self" experiences gratitude and inner serenity.

- When you remember who you really are, you can experience joy and love, even in short moments. These moments gradually become frequent in your life.

- When you are connected to your "Real Self" you lift your vibration to attract your heart's desires. This is the law of attraction.

PART II

HOW IT ALL BEGAN

HOW IT ALL BEGAN

*A*s a human being you are made up of a body, mind, spirit and emotions. The body is the physical self, the mind is your thoughts, the spirit is your connection to your source, and emotions are your feelings.

Let's focus on taking a look at the function of the mind. We spoke earlier of understanding that your thoughts are things which are creative and manifest realities into your life. Your thoughts also hold beliefs that judge circumstances and other people, as well as the self.

Thoughts in the mind are quite often opposed to each other. For example, you might think of doing something, and right away you hear a voice that says, "Well, on the other hand, don't do that, do this." This creates inner conflict. Daily, don't you hear voices in your head that seem to be talking to you? There can be a lot of chatter going on.

Why is this?

As a human being you were born into this world from a comfortable non-disturbed state. This is the warm and protected womb of your birth mother. Think about that existence for a moment. Quiet, warm, relaxing, calm and completely safe. You were fed consistently. You simply floated around with all of your needs met. No worries, right?

Not until that shocking day you were born. All of a sudden this newly developed baby starts to feel something is radically changing. What is happening?

Imagine this. Suddenly, for the first time things begin constricting around the little baby's body, and pushing it. And it hurts. It feels itself being plunged into bright lights and that really hurts too. There are very loud noises that this baby has never experienced. Sometimes, the baby may have even been spanked on its little bottom. It may have even had something cold and strange thrown into its eyes.

The little baby is completely confused and it cries. The baby misses the beautiful non-disturbed state it grew in. This is when the baby makes it's very first decision ever.

"The purpose of living is to be non-disturbed and comfortable all the time".

By the time you were approximately five years old, you developed a set of core beliefs. This became the conditioning of the mind and the emotions that would continue to influence your life. These beliefs were taught to you by the ways that your parents, caretakers and teachers cared for, disciplined and responded to your actions, feelings and needs. Also, in how they treated or mistreated you.

As a small child you began to experience the approval and disapproval of these authorities. When the baby smiles and laughs, it notices that people respond with delight and there is good energy. This is when the baby learns to "please". It quickly figures out that this brings attention and approval.

On the contrary, the baby notices that when it cries it gets delicious food and warm milk. Then the baby begins to notice that when it really cries at the top of its voice, someone will pick it up and offer comfort. This is when the baby learns to "complain". Thus, creating more attention for the baby.

Then something else begins to develop as the child grows a little bit older.

Perhaps while doing something that the little child enjoys, a parent may suddenly react negatively, saying that the child is bad or selfish and it must stop what it is doing.

This startles the child. After all, it was merely feeling pleasure and fun. This is the beginning of shifting away from being one's "Real Self". This is when the child is learning it must act differently on the outside than it feels on the inside.

This learned behavior will become the masks of the "False Self" also known as the conditioning. These are the masks that will cover up the "Real I" until a person wakes up and becomes conscious enough to remember who they truly are.

As this "False Self" develops, the child learns quickly that it must act differently than it feels in order to please the parents or caretakers. The child may even begin to believe that it really is bad or selfish. After all, it was just told this by someone who they trust and believe in. These decisions will affect the child for years to come.

This is the birth of the "Not I's".

The "Not I's" are the root of all conflict. This can manifest as depression, unfulfilling relationships, low self-esteem, lack of abundance and much more.

The way out is to become acquainted with these "Not I's". You must learn who they are inside of you so that you can recognize these six masks as your "False Self". As you begin to notice and observe them in your daily life, and begin to understand that this is not your true self, the "Not I's" will lose their destructive power. To do this you must learn to dis-identify with them. You do this by telling yourself, "that is a "Not I", and it is not me".

This is the only way to wake up.

JEWELS OF WISDOM
'HOW IT ALL BEGAN'

- You were born as a pure innocent being, a "Real Self" full of love and light.

- It is what you were taught as a child that created the conditioning known as the "False Self".

- The purpose of the "False Self" is "to be non-disturbed and comfortable 100% of the time."

- The purpose of the "Real Self" is to be free to experience what life brings moment to moment in order to learn and grow.

- The conditioning you learned as a child is not who you really are. It was added on to you. Who you really are is pure love.

- Based on the negative beliefs that were created in children, the conditioning called the "Not I's" was formed.

- When you are awake you can change your thoughts about anything at anytime in order to create a better feeling.

- When you are asleep you feel like a victim of life's circumstances.

PART III

WHO ARE ALL THOSE SELVES INSIDE YOU?

WHO ARE ALL THOSE SELVES INSIDE OF YOU?

*Y*ou were born as an innocent child into this world from Divine Spirit or God. You came to this earth as pure love and light. You came here as your "Real Self" knowing nothing other than pure goodness.

It is from the destructive conditioning that was added on that you began to believe the illusion of the "False Self".

It is in listening to the conditioned mind and believing those thoughts that has caused the pain and conflicts in life. Without question, you were buying into this false illusion of who you really are. Think of particular times when you have experienced any of the following situations.

Fighting with loved ones and making things even worse. Holding your feelings inside and then feeling resentments stack up. Feeling alone in this world.

Feeling like a pretender and that other people are better and smarter than you. Experiencing feelings of insecurity and guilt. Thinking that you just can't do anything right. Feeling like you aren't enough.

Feeling like you don't matter. Feeling fearful.

Thinking that you do all the work in your relationship and feeling like a victim. Have you experienced relationships with power plays and passive aggressive behaviors? One minute they are sweet as can be and then they switch on a dime, and are blaming you? Have you felt like you are right and everyone else is wrong?

Do you ever feel like you give more than you get back? Do you find yourself stretching the truth to impress others? Blaming other people? Do you believe that they do know better but still won't change? Do you sometimes feel defensive? Do you ever experience any feelings of inner conflict, poor health, fear and insecurity? The biggest of all, do you ever feel like a victim?

All of those kinds of feelings come from the "Not I's" within you. Until you wake up to understanding these masked personalities, you will live life experiencing harmful emotions. With the "Not I's" running the show, you are living in reaction to the events, circumstances and people in your life. It is in waking up to noticing the "Not I's" and the awareness of the "Real Self" that you can begin to take charge and create a life of love, joy and ease.

Who exactly are the "Not I's"? They are the sneaky little culprits that live in the mind that have tricked you into believing they are real. This is why they are called "Not I's", as they are not real and they are not you.

These six false masked personalities are separated into two groups of three.

The Pleaser	The Complainer
The Believer	The Defender
The Pretender	The Blamer

Imagine your mind having two sides. The first group of "Not I's" lives on one side in your mind, and the second group lives on the other side. They are at opposition. They are at constant war with each other. This is what creates inner conflict. Here is what each "Not I" has to say about its purpose.

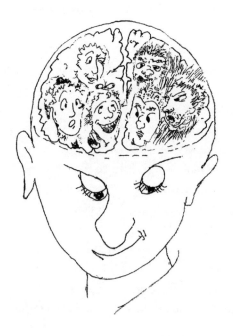

The PLEASER says, "To get what I want, I must please them".

The BELIEVER says, "I must believe and do what they say".

The PRETENDER says, "I must be different than I am. I must act differently than I feel".

From the second group:

The COMPLAINER says, "I must have my own way now and the way to get it is to complain".

The DEFENDER says, "I must stick up for my rights".

The BLAMER says, "If only he, she, it and they were different, then I could be happy".

You can see from their job descriptions that these little masks can stir up quite a lot of problems and conflict in your life.

Because the two groups of "Not I's" are in direct opposition to each other, the mind often cannot decide what to do. For example, you may unconsciously ask yourself, "in order to get what I want, is it better to please or to complain in this situation?"

This is when one side of the mind is telling you one way of looking at something, and the other side is suggesting you do something else. Thoughts just keep swaying back and forth until finally a "Not I" wins and an action is taken.

Yes, there certainly can be a lot of chatter going on!

"I seem to have an awful lot of people inside me."

- Dame Edith Evans

A very interesting aspect to understanding the "Not I's" and their job descriptions is that the first group, the PLEASER, the BELIEVER, and the PRETENDER want to make you feel diminished and guilty.

These three "Not I's want to avoid any feelings of disapproval. This is their main fear, and they will do whatever it takes to avoid it. This is why they aim to please so that others will like and approve of them. They are experts at pretending and acting as if they are in agreement with other people even when they are not. They prefer to go along with the crowd, and whatever others want.

The second group of "Not I's, the COMPLAINER, the DEFENDER, and the BLAMER want to make you feel angry and resentful.

These three "Not I's" in the second group are strongest at wanting you to feel that they are always right. Their main fear is that they will appear to be wrong and they will do whatever it takes to avoid this feeling. They always want to look good.

These two opposing sides are constantly at war with each other. They each want to win. They can drive you crazy and create much chaos and conflict particularly in relationships. This happens to be their favorite playground and is where they thrive.

THE BATTLE OF THE "NOT I's"

Are you beginning to see the dynamics at play here? As thoughts go back and forth in the mind, it is impossible to win either way. You can never feel inner peace.

Here is another interesting aspect. It is quite common for a person becoming newly acquainted with the personalities of the "Not I's" to realize that they tend to live more on one side of the mind than the other. This is expressed through a person's behaviors, feelings and emotions.

As a generalization, sometimes girls are raised to believe that they have to act lady like. They are taught to be nurturing, helpful and polite even when they do not feel like it. Therefore, in general, women tend to operate more from the first group of "Not I's" on the PLEASER side.

Whereas, boys are often raised not to show their feelings. That it is better to act tough and defend themselves. Think back to when you were a kid in elementary or middle school. It was fairly common for boys to announce that they would be fighting each other after school. Many students gathered to watch egging them on. Most males have been taught to be proud to be tough and even at times to be bullies. In general, males tend to live more in the second group of "Not I's" on the DEFENDER side.

In the following chapter we will meet the "Not I's" and hear what they actually have to say.

JEWELS OF WISDOM "WHO ARE ALL THOSE SELVES INSIDE YOU?"

- Who are the "Not I's"? They are the sneaky little voices that live in the mind and have fooled you into believing they are real.

- The Six "Not I's" are divided into two groups, living on each side of the mind. They are in constant conflict with each other.

- When you identify with the "Not I's" you are asleep. When you realize the "Not I's" are not who you really are, you are awake and conscious.

- Anytime you feel like a victim you know the "Not I's" are in charge.

- When you are asleep and the "Not I's" are running the show you're usually in "reaction" to the events, circumstances and people in your life.

- It is in becoming aware of your "Real Self" that you can begin to take charge and create a life of love, joy and ease.

PART IV

MEET THE "NOT I's"

THE PLEASER

THE PLEASER

*T*he PLEASER says, "To get what I want, I must please them". "I am the Pleaser. I smile a lot. I always try to please others so they will like me and believe that I am a good person. But, the truth is I always have a "motive". Mostly it is to avoid the pain associated with anyone disapproving of me.

I admit that sometimes when I please others and they don't appreciate it, I get resentful and want to make them pay. Oh yeah, I'll get even with them.

Oh, and I also can't stand any kind of rejection…ever!

Also, I especially don't like to be ignored. I can quite easily feel deeply hurt when someone turns their back on me and walks away. That is when I want to try even harder and be even nicer.

I know that at times I can get carried away and overly please, and give too much. I have been told that I tend to be gushy or sickening sweet and that can turn other people off. The truth is, I just can't help myself.

I do give lots of compliments and I am also a great helper too. I just really want you to like and approve of me. That is all I care about.

By the way, thank you so much for reading about me. I really really do appreciate it very much".

THE BELIEVER

THE BELIEVER

The BELIEVER says, "I must believe and do as my authorities tell me."

"I am the Believer. When I was a young child growing up, I caught on real fast that if I did exactly as I was told by my parents that things went pretty smoothly for me. I also learned that when I didn't do as I was told, things didn't work out so well. Like the time I got my allowance taken away. And, I never liked getting spanked.

The same was true with my teachers. I listened carefully and they really knew what they were talking about. After all, they were really smart and educated. They knew exactly what I should do and learn.

Later, it was with my friends that I liked believing just about everything that they believed. I felt quite a bit of social peer pressure back then. You know, I am very open and flexible.

As I have grown up, I have still found that when I agree with other people's opinions and what they believe, things just go smoother for me. It's much easier to go along with their ideas. Don't rock the boat.

One thing I am most excited about is when I read magazine ads. I mean, they are actually promising me that if I owned that cool car, that maybe, just maybe I could have a beautiful girlfriend like the one in the ad. I know! It's fantastic!

Recently, while watching the game, I saw a really great commercial. It actually suggested that if I drink their brand that I would have tons of friends and yet, even another beautiful girlfriend. I absolutely cannot wait to get to the store to buy it!"

THE PRETENDER

THE PRETENDER

*T*he PRETENDER says, "I must be different that I am. I must act differently that I feel".

"I am the Pretender. I am constantly comparing myself to other people. I often feel like they are smarter and much better looking. Certainly they are more successful than me.

I can be highly critical of myself. I am constantly judging and analyzing the things that I do and how I look. I just can't stand to feel inadequate in any way. I can be quite the perfectionist.

Also, I find making things up as I go along keeps me feeling pretty darn powerful. Telling little white lies and telling people what they want to hear can be very satisfying.

I mean, I do understand this isn't being very authentic and is probably wrong to behave this way, but it just works best for me. There I go, criticizing myself again.

I do give a lot of compliments to other people, even when I don't believe they're true. What's wrong with that? It seems to make them feel good plus I like it when they think I'm charming. I am you know!

I must admit though, at times it can be quite exhausting having to keep up a front, when I feel so differently inside. It can cause me to feel quite a lot of anxiety.

It is very important for me to look successful to others. I often brag about my accomplishments, mostly things I did in the past. You do like me when I do this, right"?

THE COMPLAINER

THE COMPLAINER

The COMPLAINER says, "I must have my own way now and the way to get it is to complain".

"I am the Complainer. I tend to worry a lot. Not only for myself, but for other people too. There is just so much wrong in the world. Everywhere I look I see how things should be different. It's just not fair sometimes.

It's true that I do feel like a victim quite often. But I know that I am always right and I pretty much know what is best for everyone else. I just have a knack.

One thing that irks me the most, is how much I do for other people and they just don't appreciate me. This is very upsetting to me. It happens a lot.

So many things are awful. There is so much to truly complain about. Like the weather, bad service in restaurants, politics and the economy, and mainly in my relationships. Just turn on the news and there it is. It's endless.

I am actually very good at complaining. There are so many ways to indulge myself. I do enjoy the obvious ways of complaining by just telling it straight out like is. But, other more subtle ways I have found are my favorite. Just using my facial expressions and rolling my eyes, or a certain tone in my voice can get excellent results.

What do I enjoy most about complaining? First, I thoroughly enjoy getting my own way. I also find that most people just don't know as much as I do about the way things ought to be. It frustrates me, and I just must let them know. After all, that is my job!"

THE DEFENDER

THE DEFENDER

*T*he DEFENDER says, "I must stick up for my rights".

"I am the Defender. I enjoy debates in my relationships. I especially like arguing. It gives me the opportunity to prove how I know I am always right. It makes me feel powerful and I like to win. I cannot stand to lose!

In fact, I'll let you in on a little secret. Sometimes I actually stir things up intentionally, just so I can have the opportunity to defend myself. This is how I can be sure to get what I want.

After all, I really do not respect anyone but myself. My points of view and opinions always matter more than anyone else's. I absolutely do not respect anyone that can't see things my way, ever. I never apologize or say I am sorry.

Fact is, I just know that I'm right. End of story.

I totally hate taking responsibility for anything. That can be such a burden on me. I avoid it at all costs. I have been told that I live in denial about reality in order to not take responsibility for myself. Whatever.

One of the best parts of my job is 'explaining'. I am very good at this. I can drone on for hours to really get my point across. It is one of my best talents.

I am not always honest, that's for sure. But, that doesn't matter as long as I get my way. After all, I am totally entitled!"

THE BLAMER

THE BLAMER

*T*he BLAMER says, "If only he, she, it and they were different, then I could be happy".

"I am the Blamer. I realize that I am completely a victim of circumstances in my life all of the time. If I could control the world I would. But, because I can't do that it sure is a relief to know that nothing is my fault.

This happens to be true across the board, but especially in my relationships. If they would just do things my way, then I could just relax and be totally happy. I must constantly remind them of this.

Do you know what I find completely frustrating? It is knowing that they do know what is right, yet, they do wrong anyway. They can be so stupid and ridiculous.

I simply know how things ought to be. Actually, for just about everything. I am fortunate to be superior.

Truth be told, nothing is ever my fault. How great is that?

There are many ways that I do my job very well. Mostly, just focusing on the fact that I am better than everyone else and that nothing is my fault gives me great motivation. I truly love my job!"

NOW WHAT?

*W*ell, there you have it. You have now met the cast of characters, the six false personalities that have been running the show. They have convinced you throughout your life that they are real and that they are who you really are. The good news is discovering that they are not the real part of you. And that there are definitely solutions, tools and answers to waking up to your true self and having a life filled with love, joy and ease.

The "Not I's" are responsible for every bit of chaos and conflict ever experienced. As noted earlier, they thrive especially in relationships. For this is where human beings tend to be most vulnerable in their desire for emotional safety.

It is within relationships that the "Not I's" tend to be the most active. Imagine the following scenario. You have the "Not I's" at war in your mind, and the other person in your relationship has their own "Not I's" as well. Now, the "Not I's" can have an absolute field day. Let the "Not I" parties begin! And sadly enough, they have done just that.

Now, it's time for the good news. Let's learn the ways in which you can create a new and much more fulfilling way to live. It's time now to know the truth of who you really are.

JEWELS OF WISDOM
MEET THE "NOT I's"

- Below are the "Not I" personality combinations that oppose each other and create inner conflict.

  The PLEASER and The COMPLAINER
  The BELIEVER and The DEFENDER
  The PRETENDER and The BLAMER

- Remember, these are the two sets of "Not I's" on each side of the mind and they are directly at war with each other.

- The "Not I's" are not the real part of you. Dis-identifying with them when you notice one will cause them to lose their power.

- When you catch yourself blaming or complaining and notice a "Not I", say to yourself, "That is a "Not I", that is not me". Say, "Hi "Not I" and let it go.

- You have now met each of the "Not I's" personally. As you get acquainted with their personalities you can begin to see that they are clearly created from the conditioning of your childhood.

- It is within personal relationships that the "Not I's" thrive and can be the most active and destructive.

PART V

MEET THE "REAL SELF"

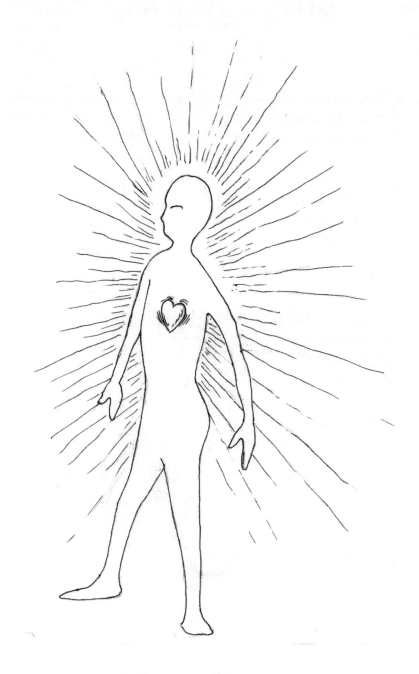

MEET THE "REAL SELF"

MEET THE "REAL SELF"

"*I* am your "Real Self". I am also referred to as your true self, the divine self, your authentic self and your spiritual self. I am your connection to God and love. I am the bright light being that is who you really are.

I live inside of your heart. Even in the times that you forget, I am still always there within you.

I am the voice that guides you when you are quiet and listen. I am the one that nudges and whispers to you. I am the one that knows. I am your intuition.

When you take the time to pray, meditate and get quiet, it is through me that God or your Higher Self answers you. I am your guiding light.

I am always with you. I am the part of you that lives your life consciously aware and awake.

I am the part of you that loves others unconditionally and without expectations or judgment.

I am pure love. I am you. This is who you really are.

Always remember this.

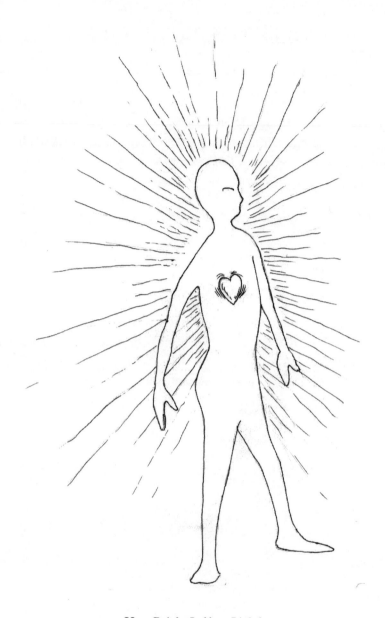

How Bright Is Your Light?
How Many Watts Are You Allowing Yourself to Shine?

Shine On "Real I"
Be Bright
You Are A Bright
Beautiful Light Being!

"There is nothing more beautiful than a human being when they begin to wake up".

- Unknown

You are becoming aware that the "Real Self" is always there within you. The conditioning that was added on is the "False Self" known as the "Not I's".

Your "Real Self" is true love and light.

The "False Self" is fear, darkness and shadows.

You are always coming from either fear or love. You have a choice, every moment of everyday to remember who you really are, and to choose love.

It is valuable to remember the "Not I's" have been in charge for a very long time. Becoming awakened is a process. It is good to understand that it takes practice and it takes time. Be patient. It is important to be easy and gentle with yourself.

In his book, *Real Magic*, Dr. Wayne Dyer reminds us "that we are a spiritual being having a human experience".

This means there will still be times that you will go to sleep, forgetting who you really are. This is okay as it is a process of remembering. It is in beginning to simply notice these moments, that awakening begins and continues. Every moment of awakening and awareness is accumulative and you always grow.

Awakening becomes like cracks of light rays that begin to stream through. Until one day, you are a beautiful beam of light shining bright most of the time.

THE VELVETEEN RABBIT

*T*here is a beautiful story that was written many years ago. In this book the author illustrates what "waking up" may look like. It is from a book entitled *The Velveteen Rabbit.*

The Velveteen Rabbit is a children's novel by Margery Williams and illustrated by William Nicholson. Originally published in 1922, the story chronicles the tale of a toy stuffed rabbit and its quest to become real through the love of his owner, a small boy.

The small boy receives a Velveteen Rabbit stuffed animal for Christmas. Following is an excerpt from this classic story about two toys talking with each other, wondering about becoming real rather than being toys.

One day, while talking with the Skin Horse, the Velveteen Rabbit learns that a toy can become real if its owner really loves it. The Skin Horse makes the Velveteen Rabbit aware that "…once you are Real you can't become unreal again. It lasts for always.

The VELVETEEN RABBIT

By Margery Williams

with illustrations by William Nicholson

"What is REAL?" asked the Velveteen Rabbit one day... "Does it mean having things that buzz inside you and a stick-out handle?"

"Real isn't how you are made," said the Skin Horse. "It's a thing that happens to you." "When someone loves you for a long time, not just to play with, but REALLY loves you, then you become Real".

"Does it hurt?" asked the Rabbit.

"Sometimes", said the Skin Horse, for he was always truthful. "When you are Real you don't mind being hurt".

"Does it happen all at once, like being wound up?" he asked, "or bit by bit?"

"It doesn't happen all at once", said the Skin Horse. "You become. It takes a long time. That's why it doesn't happen to people who break easily or have sharp edges, or have to be carefully kept.

Generally, by the time you are Real, most of your hair has been loved off, and your eyes drop out and you get loose at the joints and very shabby. But these things don't matter at all, because once you are Real you can't be ugly, except to people who don't understand...once you are Real you can't become unreal again. It lasts for always."

Even though this sweet story was written for children, you can see the beautiful metaphor of the power of love and waking up to knowing your "Real Self". It is a valuable reminder to read at any age, for both children and adults.

In the story the Rabbit asks the Skin Horse, "does becoming real hurt?" And the Skin Horse replies, "yes, sometimes it is painful". The process of waking up can be very uncomfortable for a period of time.

Growth as we know by nature is often painful. Think of a little seed planted in the ground under the earth. As it begins to grow, it pushes against the resistance of the soil. And this is not easy. In spite of its discomfort, the seed continues stretching and growing, all the time reaching for the light. With the seed's intention of becoming a flower, it continues becoming stronger until it pushes through to a world of beautiful and warm sunlight. Here it continues to grow and flourishes into a beautiful flower.

You could say the metaphor of the seed is much like the human process of waking up.

It is in our desire and determination to be awake that we can eventually find ourselves living a life of joy and fulfillment.

"Every blade of grass has its angel that bends over it and whispers, grow, grow".

-The Talmud

JEWELS OF WISDOM
"MEET THE REAL SELF"

- Take time each day to sit quietly and listen. You will receive guidance from your inner spirit, your "Real Self".

- Who you really are is pure love and light. Feel the joy and let your light shine bright.

- You are always coming from either a place of fear or love. It is a choice.

- Your "Real Self" will be there for you, even in the moments that you forget. You can awaken over and over.

- "You are a spiritual being having a human experience". Be easy and gentle with yourself.

- Begin to notice when you see a "Not I" in yourself. This is the beginning of waking up. Just observe.

- Waking up to remembering who you really are isn't always comfortable, and often painful. Yet, it is so worth it. You will have more serenity, love and joy.

- Your "Real Self" within you loves unconditionally and sees the "Real Self" in others, even when they forget who they really are.

- You can always return to love in any given moment. This is who you are.

PART VI

"THE WAY OUT"
TOOLS FOR
TRANSFORMATION

"Waking up is not a matter of chance…it's a matter of choice."

-Rose Blackham

THE TOOLS

What To Know:

*T*he more that you awaken the "Not I's" become threatened for their existence.

They have been in charge and running the show for a very long time, and they do not want to give up their jobs now or their power over you.

They want to keep you asleep so that they can continue to do their jobs of creating conflict. The light that shines within you is their biggest threat. They will do anything to try to stop you from waking up. They are stubborn and they are sneaky.

They have been responsible for all the conflict you have experienced in your life…up to now.

They thrive best and crawl out of their dark shadows especially when you are stressed and exhausted.

They rear their little masked heads when you are overly hungry or tired. This only empowers them. They love it when you are out of balance in any way. This is when they sneak in easily. Relationships are their favorite playground.

As you develop more awareness of your "Real Self" and "False Self", the "Not I's" become afraid of losing their power and control.

It is not uncommon to find that as a person begins to wake up and notice the "Not I's", that they seem to be louder than ever. They are fighting for their lives. Because they live in the dark shadows of the mind, there is nothing that threatens them more than the light.

What To Do:

Be mindful that you cannot force the "Not I's" to disappear or just go away. In fact, the more you try to do this, the stronger they become.

There is an answer. Here is the key solution to disempowering the destructive "Not I's".

Become an observer. In fact, become a very good one. This is the quickest way to take charge over them.

You do this by learning to dis-identify with them as much as possible. Anytime you notice that you are feeling like a victim, you know they are there.

This is the time to tell yourself, "That is a "Not I", that is not me". Just realize that you fell asleep. By becoming the observer your "Real Self" is present and you are once again awake.

This is a process. This is the work. It is important that it be repetitive. Notice the "Not I's" as much and as often as you can. This is how they lose their power.

What to Remember:

It is one step at a time. Waking up and falling asleep over and over again are all part of this process. Just continue to observe, notice the "Not I's" whenever possible and detach. Be gentle and easy with yourself.

This is the way that your beautiful light begins to shine brighter. This is the answer to living a life of ease and serenity.

Here is some very good and promising news. ***You never lose any progress that you have made. It is always accumulative.***

FORGIVENESS

GRATITUDE

SELF-CARE

THE POWER OF PLAY

FORGIVENESS

*F*orgiveness is one of the most healing tools. Use it often. When you find that you have fallen back asleep and perhaps reacted badly in a relationship or a situation, forgive yourself as quickly as you can. It is okay. You can start again every moment.

Forgive other people in your life when you see that they are asleep. Do not judge them. See behind their "Not I" mask. See the light in them when they forget who they really are. Forgive them when they are reacting or behaving in ways that tell you they are asleep. Observe their "Not I's" and tell yourself, "that isn't who they really are, that is their "Not I's".

It is learning about the power of the "Not I's" that you can have more compassion for yourself and for others. Jesus said on the cross, "Forgive them Father, for they know not what they do". The meaning here is the same in the sense, that while a person remains asleep and the "Not I's" are in charge, that person is merely reacting automatically from old conditioning. They too, know not what they do. Have compassion and choose love whenever possible.

Now, as for the "Not I's" themselves, it is a bit trickier. As you begin to get better at dis-identifying with them, you may at some point even find forgiveness for them. They have simply been doing their jobs. The jobs that they were designed to do. Thank them, forgive them and let them now go.

"The first step in forgiveness is the willingness to forgive. If you can state, despite your resistance, your willingness to see the spiritual innocence, the light in the soul of one who has harmed you, you have begun the journey to a deep and unshakable peace".

-Course in Miracles

GRATITUDE

*G*ratitude is another powerful healing tool. A valuable thing to remember is that a person cannot be in a state of feeling conflict and gratitude at the same time. It is not possible. Therefore, when you are feeling grateful you know you are awake.

The same can be said that when you are awake you are living in gratitude. There is love and light in your heart. When you are feeling grateful for those things that are meaningful to you, the universe cannot help but attract and bring more of all the good things that your heart desires.

It is easy to feel grateful when life is going well and things are going the way you want them to. A greater challenge is to still find gratitude when you are experiencing difficult times in your life. These are the times to look for the jewels for they are always there. This isn't always easy, but when you can do this, you will recognize how life's experiences bring personal growth and a return to gratitude.

At these times of suffering you are more likely to go to sleep and feel hurt, confused or resentful thinking that this is natural. This is when you know the "Not I's" have taken over. Gratitude is the last thing that might occur to you in such a moment. You can always choose how to look at every situation. There is always a beautiful lesson. It is all in your perspective.

> "Anything that annoys you is teaching you patience. Anyone who abandons you is teaching you how to stand up on your own two feet. Anything that angers you is teaching you forgiveness and compassion. Anything that has power over you is teaching you how to take your power back. Anything you hate is teaching you unconditional love. Anything you fear is teaching you courage to overcome your fear. Anything you can't control is teaching you how to let go."
>
> -unknown

The truth is that every situation does have a jewel, but you have to look for it. It is first a conscious intention that creates a perspective to look for the good in your life. With gratitude you get more of what you are grateful for. When you complain you get more of what you complain about. Experiencing bouts of gratitude is also known to reduce anxiety and depression. Having gratitude strengthens relationships and your own sense of well-being.

Dr. Emmett E. Miller, M.D. said, "That whether we feel gratitude and fullness or loss, deprivation and resentment there is a corresponding internal chemical state that is created in the body". He said, "Grateful people heal faster".

A feeling of gratitude evokes feelings of love and peace. This is the "Real Self". This is who you really are. This is living heaven on earth.

What many people find value in is practicing daily prayer. By starting your day with a morning prayer to God being thankful for what is in your heart. This could be as simple as for a warm bed to sleep in, a safe home to live in and for your family and anything else meaningful to you. Also ending your day with a prayer of gratitude creates a certain vibration that allows a more restful sleep.

Look at the world around you and the people in your life, and find as many ways to feel grateful as you can for the grace and many blessings you do have. Practice awareness throughout your day for even the smallest of things to be thankful for.

When you want what you have...you will always have what you want.

> "Gratitude unlocks the fullness of life. It turns what we have into enough and more. It turns denial into acceptance, chaos into order, confusion into clarity. It can turn a meal into a feast, a house into a home, a stranger into a friend. Gratitude makes sense of our past, brings peace for today and creates a vision for tomorrow."
>
> - Melodie Beattie

SELF-CARE

*T*he most important relationship you will ever have is with yourself. It is the foundation for having satisfying, balanced and loving relationships. Many people have become experts at doing a great job of taking care of everyone else. They often neglect themselves.

The "Not I's" come out to play when you are tired, stressed, hungry and out of balance. There is a high value in practicing self-care into your life.

In this fast paced world we live in today, the energy on the planet has never been more accelerated. We experience and enjoy the amazing benefits of today's technology such as computers, smart phones and social media. These things often create a huge amount of distractions.

People are rushing through life more than ever. And many are addicted to the cell phone, checking it constantly. It is easy to see this when you look around.

By practicing self-care personal rituals you are creating a center and balance in your life. When taking care of your body, mind, spirit and emotions becomes a daily priority, you will awaken a new powerful energy within. Self-care will have a positive impact on every aspect of your life.

Self-care can look different and be defined in a personal and unique way for each individual. Your life is supposed to feel good to you. Start by making a list of the things that make you feel good. Your self-care regime doesn't have to be time consuming. If you are asking yourself; "How and where can I afford to find the time to do this?" The answer is you cannot afford not to. A good place to start is doing something special each day for your body, mind, spirit and emotions. Even if you only have a few minutes, you will feel the benefits. Self-care is an intention.

Here are a few ideas.

Body:
Eat something you really like.
Take a walk outside.
Move your body.

Turn on music and dance for a minute.
Exercise.
Stretching.
Bubble bath.
Massage.
Give yourself permission just to rest.
Put on your jammies and soft socks.
Watch a movie and eat popcorn.

Mind:
Write positive affirmations.
Play games.
Do puzzles.
Send hand written cards to friends.
Enjoy a good book.
Work on a creative project that you enjoy.
Write in a journal.
Sit and quiet the mind.
Take a moment to focus on what you are grateful for.

Spirit:
Take a few moments to meditate.
Create some quiet time for yourself.
Pause and take a few deep breaths.
Listen to music you enjoy.
Read something inspirational.
Dance to a favorite song.
Experience the beauty of nature.
Prayer.
Connect to your Higher Power.

Emotions:
Focus on thoughts that make you feel good.
Appreciate the power of music.
Express love to yourself and others.
Play with your pets.

Feel what you are grateful for.
Watch a beautiful sunrise or sunset.
Smile and laugh.
Look into the eyes of others to connect.
Ponder your dreams.

It is important to do your self-care rituals consciously and with intention. This makes all the difference in the results you will feel. Do your self-care mindfully rather than mechanically.

THE POWER OF PLAY

*Y*es, play! Playing, laughing and having fun, takes away the power of the "Not I's". They tend to get out of the way. This is because when you are playing, you are letting go, allowing and relaxed.

Playing and laughing is good not only for kids but also for adults because it releases feel good chemicals called endorphins while suppressing stress hormones and strengthening the immune system. Not only do you feel younger, playing and laughing actually slows down the aging process. Many books have been written about the importance of allowing your inner child to come out to play. Enjoying unstructured, complete time out and fun just for the sake of it is another valuable form of self-care. There does not need to be any point to the activity. Just have fun and enjoy yourself. The focus of play is not on accomplishing any goal.

In relationships, having fun, being light, laughing and playing is a great benefit. Psychologists tell us, couples that play together tends to stay together. Playing with your partner creates bonding, and adds a special energy to the relationship.

Give yourself permission to play. Have a play day once in awhile. Take time out. Playing will add more balance to your life. Play is good!

In the words of George Bernard Shaw, "We don't stop playing because we grow old; we grow old because we stop playing".

"Our
bodies
know it.
Our brains
know it.
Now science
has proven it.
Adults and
kids both
need stupid
pointless fun."

-Anonymous

JEWELS OF WISDOM "THE WAY OUT" TOOLS FOR TRANSFORMATION

- Remember that the "Not I's" get threatened and sneakier the more you wake up.

- To disempower the "Not I's", become an "observer". Noticing them is the quickest way to dis-identify with them.

- Waking up is not a matter of chance…it is a matter of choice.

- In the process of waking up you never lose any progress that you have made. It's accumulative.

- Forgiving yourself, and others, as well as the "Not I's" is the doorway to waking up.

- You cannot be in a state of feeling fear and gratitude at the same time ever. Choose gratitude.

- Remember to practice self-care often. The "Not I's" sneak in when you are tired, stressed or out of balance.

PART VII

SURPRISE! THE "NOT I's" ARE A GIFT

THE FINAL TRUTH
THE "AWAKENED" SELF

*W*ho would ever imagine? After all the havoc and conflict they have created, it turns out the "Not I's" had an important purpose all along. They have actually given you a gift of waking up. They have taught that life is happening for you, and not to you.

It may come as a surprise now to learn that you are actually able to awaken the "Not I's" to support and help you. You can experience the freedom of knowing that you no longer need to believe their little voices, or feel the conflict and pain they have created in your past.

It is truly liberating when you come to understand that the "Not I's" no longer have power over your life. You can shed those illusions and the masks from your reality. You can stand in your own positive and loving light knowing you always have choice in each moment. You can stand in your own stability in knowing the truth of who you are. You have come to understand that you are pure love and that your purpose in this life is to know this and to grow.

When you come from this "awakened" conscious place, where you once saw reacting, defending and blaming you now see and feel compassion and understanding. Where you once felt entitled and often like a victim, you now see and feel deep gratitude and divine order in all of life. And, where you once experienced fear you see and feel love.

Yes, you can even now find gratitude, love and compassion for the "Not I's". It is a paradox after all. By understanding that they were just doing their jobs to help you wake up, you can actually release them from their own conditioning. The "Not I's" take on a brand new purpose which is to make a contribution rather than create conflict. It is as if the "Not I's" awaken too. The "Not I's" then come to understand the truth of who they are. Their harmful power is then transformed and lifted into love. This is the true integration of a human being.

THE AWAKENED "NOT I's" AND THEIR NEW PURPOSES

The "Awakened" PLEASER

*T*he awakened Pleaser knows that it's true nature is in making a contribution to others and to the world. It now sees itself as an "up-lifter" and wants the opportunity to add joy to the lives of others. In this way, it can make a positive difference. It has no need for accolades or approval and understands the new motive is to be of service to others and to the community.

The "Awakened" PLEASER says, "I am an up-lifter and I choose to be of service and enjoy seeing others happy and fulfilled".

The "Awakened" BELIEVER

The awakened Believer knows that it can now listen within for guidance. It realizes that other people are always entitled to their own opinions. It now listens to it's own intuition.

The "Awakened" BELIEVER says, "I listen to my feelings and intuition for guidance in my life. I now come from conscious choice."

The "Awakened" PRETENDER

The awakened Pretender's mantra is "I am enough". It knows the value of being congruent. Which is to be the same on the inside as on the outside and live in authenticity.

The "Awakened" PRETENDER says, "I now let go of the need of any approval of others. I acknowledge myself for the loving truth of who I am. I enjoy being authentic".

The "Awakened" COMPLAINER

The awakened Complainer remembers that every challenge and situation has a jewel and focuses on that. It looks for ways to find gratitude and express appreciation. It notices what is working rather than what is not.

The "Awakened" COMPLAINER says, "I now accept the flow of life and allow others the freedom to be who they are. I express appreciation often and find gratitude daily".

The "Awakened" DEFENDER

The awakened Defender knows the value of respecting and understanding the feelings of others. It lives a life of compassion, kindness and care for all people and the world.

The "Awakened" DEFENDER says, "I choose to be understanding, be a good listener and have compassion for others".

The "Awakened" BLAMER

The awakened Blamer now takes full responsibility. It realizes that it is the creator of the circumstances in it's life through it's own thoughts and feelings.

The "Awakened" BLAMER says, "I take responsibility for myself and I see the innocence in others without judgment".

The newly awakened "Not I's" are now relieved and they feel free. They welcome and want to embrace their new jobs. They have served their old jobs and have given you a gift in assisting you to wake up to a life with a higher consciousness and awareness. Now, when conflict and resistance does arise in your life, you can hear the new voices of the awakened "Not I's". They will remind you the truth of who you and they really are, which is pure love and light.

Accept this gift of the awareness of the "Not I's" and their new conscious jobs. As you wake up to a deeper understanding of who you really are in your life, and begin to embrace this, they too wake up to a deeper level of compassion and truth now. Lovingly forgive yourself for allowing the "Not I's" to take control over your state of being, your relationships and your life. Forgive the "Not I's" for the pain, struggles and resistance they created in the past.

Have an abundance of gratitude for the privilege you have had to lovingly support the "Not I's" in their process of waking up, as they now learn how to create harmony rather than conflict.

Embrace the new opportunity and responsibility you have to assist them in every way you can. Remember, they can temporarily fall asleep again. And they will. This is the time to remember your "tools" and to simply continue to "observe" the "Not I's". This is the time to realize that is not who you really are. This is the work. This is the awareness. By practicing and remembering the new jobs of the "Not I's", you will find yourself in a more consistent state of peace, love and joy. You may want to gently remind the "Not I's" of their new jobs and thank them.

This is the true integration of a human being.

Remember that waking up is a process. When you catch yourself falling asleep know that you can start fresh again every single day.

JEWELS OF WISDOM
"SURPRISE! THE NOT I's ARE A GIFT"

- It is truly liberating to realize that the "Not I's" can no longer have power in your life.

- Having compassion for the "Not I's" allows forgiveness for yourself and for others.

- The Awakened "Not I's" new purposes are:

  The Pleaser: To make a contribution to others.
  The Believer: To listen to intuition for guidance.
  The Pretender: To live a life of authenticity.
  The Complainer: To express appreciation.
  The Defender: To be compassionate.
  The Blamer: To take personal responsibility.

- Remember now that the "Not I's" are a gift and they are there for a purpose to help you to wake-up.

- Waking up is a process. You absolutely can live as your "Real Self" most of the time and experience a peaceful state of being.

PART VIII

HEAVEN ON EARTH

HEAVEN ON EARTH

"Your beliefs become your thoughts,
your thoughts become your words,
your words become your actions,
your actions become your habits,
your habits become your destiny."

-Gandhi

Living with a sense of heaven on earth is experiencing joy filled moments, a sense of balance and well-being, and to expect miracles and see the jewel in everything. It is trusting that this beautiful universe does not make any mistakes. There is purpose and a natural flow of life when you keep gratitude in your heart everyday. Your life is supposed to feel good to you. Heaven can be here now.

Heaven on earth is living life with ease. You no longer have the desire to effort. Trust and allowing the flow of life's events and circumstances become your natural habit. Living in the present moment and keeping your mind out of the past and the future brings peace. When you are in fear your mind is the past or the future. There is no fear in the present moment.

You get what you think about. By focusing your thoughts and feelings in positive and loving energy you then will experience more of the same in your life. Whatever you think about you attract. It is important to remember the law of attraction is always working in your life whether positive or negative. If you think about what you do not want that is what you will get…more of what you do not want. If you think about what you do want you get more of that. Let's take this universal principle further.

The universe always responds to your thoughts literally. There is a powerful tool called the "as if" principle. Think of something you want to manifest in your life. Then think of that situation "as if" it already exists for you. Rather than saying "I want," replace it with saying "I now have" or "I now am" and complete the sentence with your desire.

Meditate on it and keep your thoughts focused. Create the feelings that you already have this in your life now. Your job is to simply let go and allow the universe to do its part. Trust this process. Experiment with this. You will be amazed at the miracles that show up. This is living heaven on earth.

"THE STEPS TO CREATION" THE "WHAT" AND THE "HOW" PRINCIPLE

Step One:

The "What"

Think of something you want. Your job is simply to get clear about what this is without worrying about how to make it happen. Clarity is power. You might write it down in your journal. Visualize your desire. It can be fun to look for pictures and words in magazines to create your vision board and collage that inspire you.

The "How"

This is the job of the universe. Life will figure out the "how" of manifesting your desires. You simply need to let go and allow.

Step Two:

Doing the next thing in front of you.

While letting go of trying to figure out the "how", you can still consciously move your energy in the direction of your desire. Simply focus on doing the very next thing in front of you. This keeps your mind out of the past and the future. This is empowering and you will find a sense of relief knowing you do not have to figure everything out. You can still visualize the end result and let go of the process of how to get there.

Step Three:

"Show Up, Pay Attention, Tell the Truth and Let Go".

This is a simple yet extremely powerful tool to say to your self often.

1. Show up. Be totally in the present moment.
2. Pay Attention. Focus and be aware.
3. Tell The Truth. Be real and authentic.
4. Let Go. Breathe and let go of any attachment to the outcome.

JEWELS OF WISDOM
LIVING HEAVEN ON EARTH

- Know you can live with serenity instead of conflict.

- Always see a jewel in every situation.

- Have gratitude.

- Accept "what is" as it is, instead of what you think "ought to be".

- Feel like the luckiest person in the world.

- Remember when you want what you have, you will always have what you want.

- Look for the good in other's rather than their faults or judging them.

- Give yourself permission for actions of "self-care" on a regular basis.

- Allow yourself to play often. Have fun.

- Do what makes you feel good.

THE CATERPILLAR AND BUTTERFLY CONCEPT

The Metaphor

"What the caterpillar calls the end of the world, the Master calls a butterfly".

-Richard Bach

*B*efore a caterpillar becomes a beautiful butterfly it finds itself living inside a dark and cold cocoon. The caterpillar begins to realize that it is in a process of dying. What the caterpillar imagines to be the end of its life is, in fact, actually the beginning.

This transformation is symbolic of the destructive power of the "Not I's" dying as you learn to dis-identify with them. They then take on new jobs and purposes to awaken to a new way of living. Just like the butterfly, this describes how the consciousness expands in order to wake-up.

The purpose of the birth of the butterfly is much like the birth of the "Real Self". It is in letting go of the conditioning of old beliefs and replacing them with new ones that will allow the experience and freedom of a new way of life.

To some, the caterpillar might look insignificant as compared to the beauty of a butterfly. Yet, the caterpillar is part of the evolution of the life of the butterfly. It is the same in understanding the "Not I's". At first glance they can appear to be negative until you come to learn that they are part of the evolution of your growth. The butterfly is the metaphor of waking up to your "Real Self".

The concept of the caterpillar becoming a butterfly shows the process of growth as human beings. You cannot find clarity without contrast in life. Like the caterpillar living in the cocoon, it is out of the darkness that comes light. Light is inside darkness. Remove the darkness and you have light. It is like the falling rain before the flowers grow and blossom. It is the ebb and flow of the torrent ocean waves that will soon calm to quiet and still blue waters. It is like the wind which blows to clear away the old. It is the pouring rainstorm that creates a breathtaking rainbow. There is a purpose to everything. Just as in nature where everything evolves, so are we.

Having the awareness of the "Not I's" can be empowering to see the contrast of living a life either asleep or awake. New beliefs can be replaced with old ones. Just like the moment when the butterfly takes flight, it instantly sees the world from a new perspective. It sees a wider point of view and a panorama of a beautiful world.

It is also helpful to know that when a butterfly breaks out of its cocoon it does not immediately fly away. It first learns to walk and then quickly flies in all its beautiful colored glory with its wings to the sky.

Like the butterfly, the "Not I's" will awaken slowly but surely in their own time. Continue to observe and dis-identify with them. Waking up is a lifetime process. You can wake-up and fall asleep over and over. Patience and understanding is called for during this process. Be gentle with yourself.

In the process of waking up remember that you cannot ever go back. Why would a butterfly want to crawl back into a cocoon and become a caterpillar?

> "The caterpillar dies so the butterfly could be born. And, yet, the caterpillar lives in the butterfly and they are but one".
>
> -Unknown

A Final Message From
The Real Self

My Dearest,

I have been waiting for you to awaken to the understanding and remembrance of your true identity of that who you really are. You are truly a beautiful miracle sent to this earth from God. You are a huge beacon of light that shines the love from your being out into the world. And, my dear, remember you do this simply by remembering and being who you are. Nothing more. You are whole and complete now. Let the past go and embrace today with this knowingness, that anything and everything that is unlike that of peace, love and joy are illusions that can now easily fall away forever more. You are love. And, it is in being the pure love and light that you truly are, that you will now only find more of the same. Be peace and you will find peace. Have forgiveness and you will live with ease. Find gratitude in as much as you can every day, and you will live with a heart full of deep joy. Let the love within you flow to others and you will be adding more beautiful light to the world. Trust in it, believe in it, for all of this is who you truly are and always have been. Feel the freedom and the joy of holding these knowings close to your heart now. You are love and you are loved.

Welcome Home

This is not the end, this is just the beautiful beginning.